In
1935 if you wanted to
read a good book, you needed
either a lot of money or a library card.
Cheap paperbacks were available, but their
poor production generally mirrored the quality
between the covers. One weekend that year,
Allen Lane, Managing Director of The Bodley Head,
having spent the weekend visiting Agatha Christie,
found himself on a platform at Exeter station trying to
find something to read for his journey back to London.
He was appalled by the quality of the material he had to
choose from. Everything that Allen Lane achieved from that
day until his death in 1970 was based on a passionate belief
in the existence of 'a vast reading public for *intelligent*
books at a low price'. The result of his momentous vision
was the birth not only of Penguin, but of the 'paperback
revolution'. Quality writing became available for the price of
a packet of cigarettes, literature became a mass medium
for the first time, a nation of book-borrowers became a
nation of book-buyers – and the very concept of book
publishing was changed for ever. Those founding
principles – of quality and value, with an overarching
belief in the fundamental importance of reading –
have guided everything the company has
done since 1935. Sir Allen Lane's
pioneering spirit is still very much alive
at Penguin in 2005. Here's to
the next 70 years!

MORE THAN A BUSINESS

'We decided it was time to end the almost customary half-hearted manner in which cheap editions were produced – as though the only people who could possibly want cheap editions must belong to a lower order of intelligence. We, however, believed in the existence in this country of a vast reading public for intelligent books at a low price, and staked everything on it'
Sir Allen Lane, 1902–1970

'The Penguin Books are splendid value for sixpence, so splendid that if other publishers had any sense they would combine against them and suppress them'
George Orwell

'More than a business … a national cultural asset'
Guardian

'When you look at the whole Penguin achievement you know that it constitutes, in action, one of the more democratic successes of our recent social history'
Richard Hoggart

The Bastille Falls

SIMON SCHAMA

PENGUIN BOOKS

PENGUIN BOOKS

Published by the Penguin Group
Penguin Books Ltd, 80 Strand, London WC2R ORL, England
Penguin Group (USA) Inc., 375 Hudson Street, New York, New York 10014, USA
Penguin Group (Canada), 10 Alcorn Avenue, Toronto, Ontario, Canada M4V 3B2
(a division of Pearson Penguin Canada Inc.)
Penguin Ireland, 25 St Stephen's Green, Dublin 2, Ireland
(a division of Penguin Books Ltd)
Penguin Group (Australia), 250 Camberwell Road, Camberwell, Victoria 3124,
Australia (a division of Pearson Australia Group Pty Ltd)
Penguin Books India Pvt Ltd, 11 Community Centre,
Panchsheel Park, New Delhi – 110 017, India
Penguin Group (NZ), cnr Airborne and Rosedale Roads, Albany,
Auckland 1310, New Zealand (a division of Pearson New Zealand Ltd)
Penguin Books (South Africa) (Pty) Ltd, 24 Sturdee Avenue,
Rosebank 2196, South Africa

Penguin Books Ltd, Registered Offices: 80 Strand, London WC2R ORL, England

www.penguin.com

Citizens first published by Viking 1989
Published in Penguin Books 1990
This extract published as a Pocket Penguin 2005

1

Set in 11/13pt Monotype Dante
Typeset by Palimpsest Book Production Limited
Polmont, Stirlingshire
Printed in England by Clays Ltd, St Ives plc

Contents

Two Kinds of Palace

Versailles had been built against Paris.

The first fountain to be seen in the park of the château on descending from the terrace tells the story. In a circular pool, Latona stands holding her infant boy Apollo. She has fled from the jealous wrath of Juno, whose husband Jupiter has been making advances to her. Stopping on her flight to drink some water, Latona is attacked by peasants, mobilized by the vindictive goddess. Seeing her plight, Jupiter intervenes and transforms the peasants into frogs. This is the moment at which the sculptor caught the story, with cat-sized amphibians squatting or jumping towards the nymph, croaking in their metamorphosis. Some still retain their human trunks while their heads have changed to popping eyes and broad, gaping mouths.

For the Sun King the story had direct personal significance. His mother, Anne of Austria, had been driven from Paris by the rebellion of the Fronde, carrying her infant Apollo as a fugitive. In his maturity, Louis XIV was determined never again to be held captive by the people and peers of Paris. Though the château at Versailles had begun as a hunting lodge and place of masque and revelry, the King rapidly made it the place in which he could redefine his absolutism. His minister Colbert spent enormous sums on the Louvre, hoping that Louis would make it his principal seat of government, but to no avail. To be the Sun King meant constructing a symbolic realm of stone and water, marble and mirrors, in which the monarch and the planet would traverse the course of the day serenely unoccluded by the havoc of city life. Court music would prevail over the croaking of the frogs.

For a century, the strategy worked. Paris and Versailles remained worlds apart. If the King's peace was disturbed at Versailles it was by local townsmen and peasants, for the six-hour walk from Paris was a deterrent against popular manifestations. Not only was such a journey daunting in time and distance, it was dangerous. The Bois de Boulogne, through which travelers would have to go to reach the western roads, was notoriously full of *bandes* of thieves and whores.

By carriage, however, the journey was two hours, three at the most. And in the reign of Louis XVI the center of gravity for the *grands* of the court shifted back from the château to the city. Their *hôtels* were in the faubourg Saint-Germain or expensively refurbished in the Marais, their places of recreation the Opéra, the city theaters and the *concerts spirituels*, beside which court entertainment seemed pallid and derivative. The best art was at the biennial Salon, the best talk in private dinners and 'assemblies' like those to be found chez Duport or Necker. Most important, political initiative had gravitated from the corridors and apartments of Versailles to the Palais de Justice and the Palais-Royal. So the courtiers, whose status and identity had once been defined by the pecking order at the palace, gradually became absentees. 'Even in the chains of despotism,' commented Mirabeau, 'Paris always preserved its intellectual independence which tyrants were forced to respect. Through the reign of arts and letters Paris prepared that of philosophy and through philosophy that of public morality.'

Even before Paris came to fetch the King from Versailles, the Palais-Royal had conquered the Château de Versailles. In every respect it was its opposite; indeed its nemesis. At the core of the château was a pavilion block where the King's control over business was formalized by apartments enfilading off one another so that access at each stage could be barred or yielded as ritual and decorum required. North and south extended immense half-mile wings, dependencies in every sense, that housed the governmental and palatial services of the theoretically omnipotent monarch. The Palais-Royal was an open space, colonnaded at its perimeter: a Parisian equivalent of republican spaces like the Piazza San Marco in Venice. Its architecture gave no instructions. Rather it invited sauntering, watching, browsing, reading, buying, talking, flirting, pilfering, eating – all at random – in spontaneously improvised order or in no order at all. While Versailles was the most carefully patrolled place in France, the Palais-Royal, as the property of the Duc d'Orléans, prohibited the presence of any police whatsoever unless invited in by its proprietor. If institutional Versailles set great store by the hierarchy of rank, the frantic business of the Palais-Royal subversively jumbled it up. Versailles proclaimed corporate discipline; the Palais-Royal celebrated the public anarchy of the appetites.

At court, and even to some extent in council meetings, utterances were, in all senses, guarded. In the Palais-Royal, everything could be said, and the more extravagantly the better. At coffeehouses like the Café Foy, Arthur Young watched

expectant crowds listening *à gorge déployée* to certain orators who from chairs or tables harangue their audience. The eagerness with which they are heard and the thunder of applause they receive for every sentiment of more than common hardiness or violence against the present government cannot easily be imagined.

He was just as shocked by the democratization of pyrotechnics. At Versailles, fireworks shows, since the days of Louis XIV, had been carefully constructed to pay tribute to majesty. In the Palais-Royal, courtesy of Orléans, twelve sous bought as many squibs, rockets and serpents as five livres would bring from regular sources of supply. On the night of June 27, in celebration of the reunion of the orders, the Paris sky exploded with noise and color while the heavens above Versailles remained mournfully silent.

That the Palais-Royal was the empire of liberty was no longer in doubt when mutinying companies of the *gardes françaises* went there on June 28 to announce that they would under no circumstances fire on the people. On the thirtieth, two of their number went to the National Assembly dressed in civilian clothes to denounce their commander, the Duc du Châtelet, and were arrested by hussars and sent, along with a dozen of their comrades, to the Abbaye prison. When word of the incarceration spread, they were released by a crowd of four hundred who then went on to treat the soldiers to a festive and public supper. The Duc d'Orléans opened the premises for all-night carousing, and guarded by their 'citizen-brothers' the renegade grenadiers slept on the floor of the Variétés Amusantes music hall. The next day, baskets were suspended from their new accommodation in the Hôtel de Genève inside the Palais-Royal, so that well-wishers could make patriotic contributions to their heroes. Not wanting to endorse a complete defiance of authority, the electors at the Hôtel de Ville and the National Assembly concocted a face-saving compromise by which the guards agreed to return to the prison for one night, after which they would be pardoned and discharged.

In the climate of boozy, loquacious defiance that prevailed at the Palais-Royal, it was not surprising that the Paris revolution began there. But it was born less of festive revolt than desperation. By July, bread prices were reaching levels that were symptomatic not just of dearth but of famine. Conditions throughout urban France were rapidly approaching the level of a food war. In France's second city, Lyon, at the end of June, rioters had already enforced duty-exempt sales of grain in the mistaken belief that they were doing the King's bidding. In Paris, sporadic attacks on the customs *barrières* around the city were becoming so frequent that troops had to be posted both there and at the markets and accompany all convoys to protect grain and flour. Wednesdays and Saturdays, when the itinerant bakers

sold their merchandise at Les Halles and other desig-
nated markets, were especially perilous occasions. The
bakers were forbidden to remove from their stalls unsold
loaves left at the end of the day, so it was at that time
that hungry crowds congregated in the hope of
bargains. And it was then that the danger of violence
and the seizure of loaves was most acute.

Early July was also a crisis for the poor in another
crucial respect. For at the end of its first week was the
dreaded *terme*: the date for the settlement of all bills,
including rent. As Richard Cobb so vividly describes,
the July *terme* was the worst, since by the October *terme*
the harvest would be in and bread cheaper, and in
January more clemency and credit were often extended
because of the bitter winter months. In July, prior to
the harvest, bread prices were always at their highest
and disposable income lowest. On the eve of the day of
settlement, the seventh, whole families and colonies of
families would decamp, sometimes taking with them
the sheets they used to climb down from high windows.
It was a time of fear, unsettlement and exodus.

So when the news that Necker had been summar-
ily dismissed and sent into exile by the King reached
the Palais-Royal on Sunday, the twelfth of July, it
produced an instantaneous wave of panic and fury. For
Necker had become not just a symbol of the victory
of the Third Estate, but the latest *père nourricier*. In
many of the countless prints celebrating his fame, he
was shown as the bringer of cornucopias: the man who
would make solvency from bankruptcy, create work
where there was unemployment and bring bread

where there was famine. It was his reputation for integrity that hovered over him like a halo, in direct contrast with aristocrats, who would stop at nothing, even engineering a famine, to dislodge him from power. (Not all this flattery was unmerited. Necker had put up his personal fortune as collateral for a grain shipment from the Amsterdam banking house Hope.)

The notion that famines were caused not by the climate but by conspiracy had a long pedigree in France. But it was never more widely shared nor more angrily expressed than in 1789. If bakers and millers who withheld their stock from the market to drive prices even higher were the immediate villains, behind them lay an even more sinister aristocratic cabal. Its immediate object was to discredit Necker and secure his dismissal. With him gone, so the pamphlets said, the people could be held hostage until the National Assembly was itself safely dissolved. 'Past centuries,' said the author of one pamphlet, 'can show no precedent for so foul a plot as that which this dying aristocracy has hatched against mankind.'

Sometimes, conspiracy theories turn out to be correct. There was, of course, no plot to starve the people into submission, but there certainly was a design to remove Necker and dissolve the National Assembly. On July 9, for example, opinions about Necker were expressed in strikingly different ways at Versailles and at the Palais-Royal. As he was about to enter the royal council, Necker was greeted by Artois shaking his fist at him, abusing him as a 'foreign traitor' and a 'sorry bourgeois' who had no 'place' in the council and who should go

back to the 'little city' where he belonged. In the meeting itself the Prince went so far as to tell the Minister
he thought he should be hanged. On the same day at
the Palais-Royal, a 'woman of quality' was publicly
spanked for allegedly spitting on a portrait of the hero-
minister.

All these fears and suspicions seemed corroborated by
the increasing numbers of troops in and around Paris.
Estimates of their number exaggerated the threat, but
there was no mistaking the conspicuous German and
Swiss soldiers among them. (Even some of the native
French regiments were German-speakers from Lorraine.)
Foreign troops, in coalition with bands of 'armed brig-
ands,' were commonly thought to be roaming the
countryside and poised to invade towns as the aveng-
ing arm of despotism.

Systematic military concentration was not a figment
of popular paranoia. Louis XVI had given the first of a
succession of marching orders to frontier regiments on
June 22, when he still expected the *séance royale* to abort
the National Assembly. When that policy failed, he
summoned more troops on the twenty-sixth. By the
sixteenth of July, a series of reinforcements was to bring
the complement of troops in the Paris and Versailles
region to more than twenty thousand. A conspicuous
number of the regiments – more than a third – were
foreign, many of them German-speaking. The King
claimed that troops were being mobilized to contain
potential disorders in and around Paris. But for the
Queen, Artois and the group of ministers led by Breteuil
eager to see the back of Necker, the military show of

force was to be the instrument by which the crown could recover its freedom of action.

That plan was to be frustrated by the anxiety of those entrusted with its enforcement, who feared that the chain of command was about to fall apart. There were some grounds for their fears. Throughout the 1780s the desertion rate in the French army had risen to three thousand a year. This was in spite of the savage punishment awarded to first offenders: ten runs through a gauntlet of fifty men armed with ramrods. On the second of July the British Ambassador reported that this same ordeal had been inflicted on two soldiers of the Swiss regiment of the Salis-Samade who had been colluding with mutinous *gardes françaises*. Two others were hanged.

The most serious problem was that disaffection was by no means confined to enlisted men but had seeped into the ranks of junior officers. If there was anywhere in the old regime where social reality corresponded to polemics about aristocratic monopolies and frustrated promotion, it was in the army. Guibert's reforms may have brought about some improvement in pay but they also brought with them Prussian discipline and no compromise in the reservation of commissions to the 'old' nobility. Though the Ségur law was meant to offer protection for the older, poorer nobility, the most publicized grievance remained spoiled young sons of rich dynasties being presented with regimental commissions when barely out of college. That irked career officers and the noncommissioned, who saw all hope of rising into the officer caste blocked by the new law. It was for good reasons, then, that anti-aristocratic rhetoric made headway in the junior ranks.

Privates in the regular army may have been even more receptive to identifying themselves with the citizenry of the Third Estate. Over eighty percent of them, according to Samuel Scott, had practiced another trade at some time and a surprisingly high proportion came from an urban artisan background. The royal army of the line, then, was not a peasant force at all but closer to the workers of the *faubourgs* who had sacked Réveillon's works and would make up the majority of the 'conquerors' of the Bastille. That improvised solidarity between troops and people was to be crucial on the fourteenth of July, when over fifty regular soldiers joined the people storming the fortress. But even before that date, reports of troops' reluctance to use force against grain seizures or forcible sales were becoming commonplace.

This instinctive fraternity was even more obvious among the *gardes françaises*. Until the monumental research of Jean Chagniot it was commonly thought that the guards were older, more settled among the Parisian population and often practicing trades to make up for their meager pay. We now have a quite different profile, but one which makes their vulnerability to revolutionary propaganda even more apparent. A great many of the guards were young, of provincial origins, especially from northern towns like Amiens, Caen and Lille, and far from settled. A series of reforms in the 1760s and 1770s had closed off the possibilities – open to their predecessors earlier in the century – of keeping shops or market stalls.

Half of the men were married with families, and sometimes their wives supported them. But the rank-and-file
of the military body on which the old regime most
relied to supplement the fifteen hundred or so police
was in fact rootless, impoverished and often insubordi-
nate. Among the lower officers, especially the sergeants,
there was, complained one older officer, a 'sentiment of
equality which unfortunately in the present century
mixes together all stations and ranks.' Jean-Joseph
Cathol, the son of an Auvergnat notary and a sergeant
in the guard, later said that it was in 1788 that he first
started to read the papers 'exposing the villainy of priests
and nobles' and took his newfound political truculence
into the ranks. Others who were less actively engaged
in political argument were simply borne along by the
atmosphere of opposition they found in the wine shops
where they drank and the Palais-Royal where they prom-
enaded. On the twelfth of July, for example, a cadet of
the Reinach regiment at Versailles encountered two
guards, in the company of women and evidently very
drunk, who told him, 'Come with us, money and
advancement await you in Paris.'

For whatever mixture of reasons, the Réveillon riots
were, for the *gardes françaises*, a kind of traumatic turning point after which they became truculently disin-
clined to obey orders. Increasingly too, they began to
live up to their name as native patriots. On the sixth of
July at Versailles they almost came to blows with
German-speaking hussars who had been mobilized to
intimidate the townspeople. And on the eighth Jean-
Claude Monnet, a lottery-ticket hawker, was arrested

for distributing among soldiers seditious pamphlets, one of which was an appeal to grenadiers from 'an old Comrade of the Gardes Françaises.' 'We are Citizens before Soldiers, Frenchmen before slaves' was its message.

Impressions became polarized very quickly. On one side appeared to be the Austrian Queen and her hangers-on at court, supported now by Hungarian hussars and German dragoons. Bivouacked on the Champ de Mars at the Invalides, they were preparing, it was said, to mine the Palais-Royal. Another encampment, at Saint-Denis, was organized to bombard the city from the Buttes-Montmartre. Necker's principal opponent, Breteuil, had been reported as saying in council, 'If we have to burn Paris, then Paris will burn,' and now, it seemed, they had the men and the means to do so. Standing against this satanic conspiracy were native soldiers, led by the *gardes françaises*, but with other troops ready to follow should the people be seriously threatened. At Nangis, 'near enough to Paris for the people to be politicians,' on June 30, the *perruquier* who dressed Arthur Young told him to 'be assured as we are that French soldiers will never fire on the people,' adding, 'but if they should, it is better to be shot than to starve.'

Mirabeau shared this view. 'French soldiers are not just automata . . . they will see in us their relatives, their friends and their families . . . they will never believe it is their duty to strike without asking who are the victims. . . . ?' But he expressed it, on July 8, in a speech to the National Assembly that was dark with foreboding. In a speech of prophetic power, he painted a picture of impending civil war. Though he too exaggerated – at thirty-five thousand – the number of troops between Versailles and Paris, no one could be oblivious to the artillery rumbling over roads and bridges, and the batteries being dug in that he described. Worst of all was the transparent deceit being practiced – the incorrigible vice of the old regime confronted with New Men. Have those who embarked on these follies, he asked rhetorically, 'foreseen the consequences they entail for the safety of the throne? Have they studied in the history of all peoples, how revolutions begin . . . ?'

He had touched a nerve in the Assembly. The deputies had watched, helpless and apprehensive, as tents went up, first in the Cour de Marbre, then in the great colonnaded Orangery built by Mansart on the model of a Roman circus. Pyramids of muskets stood propped up against the Doric columns. Mirabeau's eloquence gave voice to their gathering apprehension, and its peroration was greeted with waves of applause crashing over his sweaty head. When it subsided, an address was drafted to the King that spoke, only too correctly, of 'danger . . . beyond all the calculations of human prudence . . . The presence of troops [in Paris] will produce excitement and riot and . . . the first act of violence on the pretext of maintaining public order may begin a horrible sequence of evils.' Louis was asked to withdraw his troops and defuse this explosive situation.

On July 10, two days later, the King responded. He attempted to calm the Assembly's anxieties by claiming that the troops had been summoned to contain violent disorders in Paris of the magnitude of the Réveillon riots, that they were for the 'protection,' not the intimidation, of the Assembly. All this was the classic preparatory language of the military coup d'état. The King even added a gratuitous suggestion of removing the Assembly to Noyons or Soissons should 'conditions' make its work untenable at Versailles!

Only the most gullible royalist could possibly have believed him. The truth of course was that on the same day as Mirabeau's address – and possibly provoked by it – Louis XVI had decided on a test of strength: his force against that claimed by the National Assembly. It was a more decisive act and a speedier one than those urging this confrontation on him – in particular the Queen and the princes – had dared to hope for. He had had, it seems, enough of being told what was good for him and for the monarchy. His exasperation with Necker's self-righteousness had grown into something close to detestation when he had been upstaged by the Minister on June 23. At some point in his pursuit of boar, bird and roebuck, which continued unabated, Louis XVI had decided to assert the honor of the Bourbons.

He first needed the assent of Breteuil, who was to be appointed Necker's successor in the ministry that would take on the National Assembly. When that was given, the King informed the princes on the tenth. Though their military planning called for all available troops to be in place on the sixteenth, no one was going to dampen the King's new ardor for self-assertion. The weekend, moreover, was ideal for the coup. The National Assembly would not meet on Sunday and

Necker could be expedited out of the country before it had time to react.

On Saturday the eleventh, the Minister was about to begin a congenial dinner at the proper hour of three in the afternoon, when the Minister of the Navy, La Luzerne, arrived with a letter from the King. It was terse and to the point. It required Necker to remove himself *sans bruit* – in secret – from Versailles, indeed from France altogether, and return to Switzerland. Necker pocketed the note, spoke briefly to his wife and called for the carriage in which he usually took his evening drive. Around five o'clock a valise was slung into its interior; Mme Necker, still in her *tenue de soirée*, got in, followed by her husband. The coach should, by rights, have turned south towards the Mâconnais, Lyon and the Swiss frontier. Instead it traveled northeast towards Brussels, where the Neckers alighted the following day. From there he wrote a letter to the Dutch bankers Hope, assuring them that notwithstanding his dismissal the two million livres they had loaned as security for impending grain shipments to France remained good.

It was an act of an *honnête homme*, in dramatic contrast with the petulant insecurity of the monarch who had sacked him.

Spectacles: The Battle for Paris,
July 12–13, 1789

There had never been any doubt as to which attraction really pulled in the customers at M. Curtius' wax museum. *Le Grand Couvert* showed the royal family together with the Queen's brother, Joseph II, enjoying their dinner. It was the climax of a show which also featured celebrities and heroes like Voltaire and Vice Admiral d'Estaing. Each one was modeled and painted by Peter Creutz (for that was the German name he was born with), whose career was yet another of the showman-entrepreneur success stories of eighteenth-century France. Mayeur de Saint-Paul, whose book on the boulevard du Temple specialized in sneering at the low life and burlesque specialists to be discovered there, saw Curtius as a paragon of the self-made man: gifted, shrewd and, above all, industrious. Certainly he knew his market. At two sous a head Curtius was able to pack in nonstop lines of gaping visitors from every walk of life. When they had finished marveling at his skill and imagining themselves chuckling with Voltaire, sobbing with Rousseau or peeking at Marie-Antoinette preparing for bed, they could buy one of his little wax figures of 'gallants' and 'libertines' to provoke saucy giggles at home.

Emboldened by success and prosperity, Curtius did

not hesitate when the Palais-Royal began to let commercial space in 1784. He took Salon Number 7 and filled it with the same successful mix of military and cultural heroes and court scenes that had served him so well on the boulevard and in the fairs of Saint-Germain and Saint-Laurent. To cater to a slightly grander clientele, he added a dividing balustrade that created a two-price admission: twelve sous for the front, two for the rear. There he had to compete with some powerful rival attractions like the four-hundred-pound Paul Butterbrodt and worse still the scoundrel who passed off a wax model as 'the beautiful Zulima,' dead for two hundred years but miraculously preserved and available for complete inspection for a few sous. But Curtius knew how to keep abreast of the competition. He installed a ventriloquist who gave performances daily from noon till two and five till nine. And he became topical, adding heroes of the hour – Lafayette, Mirabeau, Target and, of course, the Duc d'Orléans and M. Necker.

So when he saw a crowd of a thousand making for Salon Number 7 in a state of patriotic uproar around four o'clock on Sunday the twelfth of June, he must have had a good idea who they were coming for. Surrendering the busts of Orléans and Necker, Curtius was able to deliver a little speech worthy of the best actors of the Théâtre-Français: 'My friends,' he declaimed, 'he [Necker] is ever in my heart but if he were indeed there I would cut open my breast to give him to you. I have only his likeness. It is yours.' A tremendous performance. The heads were marched off triumphantly by the cheering crowd.

All that day, the Palais-Royal had been a boiling pot of agitation. The King and his advisers had thought a Sunday the optimal time for news of Necker's exile to become public (as they realized, for all their secrecy, it must), since it precluded an immediate response by the National Assembly. But for the unofficial center of opposition – the Palais-Royal – Sunday was the perfect day for organized histrionics. It was packed with sightseers, *flâneurs*, orators, peasants from the villages *hors des murs*, artisans from the *faubourgs*. Around three o'clock a crowd of six thousand or so milled about a young man, pale-faced and dark-eyed, his hair spilling freely onto his shoulders, shouting excitedly from one of the tables in front of a café.

Camille Desmoulins was then twenty-six years old, the favored son of a large family from Guise in Picardy. His father, a lieutenant-colonel of the local *bailliage*, had scrimped and saved to send the precocious boy to Paris for his education. And his siblings contented themselves with careers as junior officers in the army, modest marriages and, in the case of one sister, the inevitable nunnery. Desmoulins had gone to the Lycée Louis-le-Grand, where he encountered Maximilien Robespierre from Arras and a great mix of boys – some aristocratic, many bourgeois, some even from artisan backgrounds – who made up the student population of that extraordinary institution. Like them he had drunk deep of Cicero, Tacitus and Livy, had felt Roman stirrings in his blood.

Though his father hoped he would be destined for the law, Desmoulins tried to survive from occasional writings, producing, for his effort, an 'Ode to the Estates-General.' In June 1789 *La France Libérée* (France Liberated) was accepted by the publisher Momoro, who liked to style himself 'The First Printer of Liberty.' Though it was not published until a few days after the fall of the Bastille, Desmoulins' tract is a fine example of the breast-beating, sob-provoking declamation then in vogue at the Palais-Royal. From the first lines its manner assumes an audience rather than a readership:

Listen, listen to Paris and Lyon, Rouen and Bordeaux, Calais and Marseille. From one end of the country to the other the same, universal cry is heard . . . everyone wants to be free.

It was through the voice, rather than the eye, that the apostles of liberty would rally their troops. For while the eye seduced, the voice disciplined. As a young habitué of the Palais-Royal, Desmoulins was particularly preoccupied with sexual temptation as a potent weapon of royal and aristocratic corruption. Monarchy, he wrote, tries its best to deprave us in order to 'enervate the national character and bastardize us by surrounding our youth with places of seduction and debauchery and besieging us with prostitutes.'

This Machiavellian design would be thwarted, for in the capital alone there were more than thirty thousand men ready to abandon their *délices* to unite themselves, 'at the first signal, with the sacred cohorts of the *patrie*.' Already, they had taken command of the theater of eloquence. 'Only Patriots now raise their voices. The enemies of the public good are silenced or, if they dare to speak . . . immediately mark themselves for the penalty of their felony and their treason.'

Drawing on his schoolboy exercises in the classics, Desmoulins used in his peroration the same tone of Virtue Militant, but for extra effect added the patriotic martyrdom exemplified in neoclassical history paintings in the Salon and on the stage. Blood was important in these likenesses. Desmoulins compared himself with the fallen warrior Otyrhades, who wrote 'Sparta has triumphed' in his own blood on a captured standard. 'I who have been timid now feel myself to be a new man [so that] I could die with joy for so glorious a cause, and, pierced with blows, I too would write in my own blood "France is free!"'

So Desmoulins had already scripted the performance he would give to such rousing effect before the crowd at the Café Foy on July 12. He wrote to his father that, on arriving at the Palais-Royal at about three, he joined with some fellows all urging citizens to take arms against the treachery that had removed Necker, 'whom the Nation had asked to be preserved.' A creature of impulse (obedient thus to Nature, not Culture), he jumped onto a table, his head 'suffocating under a multitude of ideas' which he vocalized without any respect for order. Of Necker, he said a monument should be erected, not an exile decreed. 'To arms, to arms and [plucking leaves from a chestnut tree] let us all take a green cockade, the color of hope.' At that moment Desmoulins thought he saw police arrive – or so he claimed. The suspicion allowed him to pose as the imminent victim of tyranny. A new Saint Bartholomew's Eve massacre impended, he warned: a reference point that was already becoming an important cliché of Patriot rhetoric and which would be reinforced by the most popular play of 1789: Marie-Joseph Chénier's *Charles IX*. Pointing to his breast with one hand and waving a pistol in the other (another piece of stage business that would become standard in the Convention), Desmoulins defied the stooges of tyranny: 'Yes, yes, it is I who call my brothers to freedom; I would die rather than submit to servitude.'

The audience response was gratifying. Desmoulins was an instantaneous hero, surrounded by arms clasping him, shouts of 'bravo,' kisses, fiery oaths never to abandon his side. He was moved off amidst a great shouting and cheering throng that seized anything green that might be available – ribbon, leaves, whole branches: a small army in search of heroes and guns.

The heroes were missing in person: Necker at Brussels, Orléans playing in his own amateur theatricals at Saint-Leu. (Learning of the Paris revolt, one of his company, a painter named Giroux, rode posthaste still costumed as Polyphemus the Cyclops and was nearly roughed up by a crowd at the *barrière* who assumed his one eye to be the sinister mark of a police spy.) But Curtius could supply proxy *personnages* in wax. What they lacked in eloquence they more than made up for in portability and forbearance of conduct which their real personas might not have so wholeheartedly approved.

Theater had moved from its customary space onto the street. There, it was in deadly earnest and moved immediately to impose its serious drama on the world of mere *divertissement* (entertainment). Audiences were now required to give the Revolution their full attention. So a crowd of some three thousand invaded the Opéra, where Grétry's *Aspasie* was about to get under way, declaring the day one of mourning for the loss of Necker. Other theaters, especially those in the Palais-Royal and the boulevard du Temple, closed themselves without further invitation. *Agents* of the Bourse nearby announced the Exchange would remain shut on Monday, the following day, thus lending a fresh element of financial alarm to the accumulating sense of crisis. Like Desmoulins, many of the actors in this drama suddenly felt themselves to be framed within a brilliantly lit Historical Moment. Everything they did or said took on weight as though it were being chronicled by a new Tacitus even as it was being enacted. This self-conscious gravity became even more pronounced as the procession, now some six thousand strong, raised black banners and donned black coats and hats to signify the funereal seriousness of the occasion.

None of this might have mattered very much to the authorities had not the speeches, shouting and bells been accompanied by the demand for arms. It was apparent to the Baron de Besenval, who was now responsible for military command in Paris and the region, that the six thousand sundry units of police – the thousand guards; the Guêt constabulary; the crossbowmen and harque-busiers in their ceremonial pantaloons and the handful of *maréchaussées* (stationed outside the city limits) – could not possibly cope with the gathering tumult. Regular troops were stationed at Saint-Denis, Sèvres, Saint-Cloud and within the city at the Invalides, the Ecole Militaire, in the place Louis XV and on the Champs Elysées. On the Champ de Mars that same morning, before the news about Necker reached Paris, women had danced with Hungarian hussars of the Berzcheny regiment. Hours later the men were lined up in battle order. Four pieces of cannon had been moved to the Pont Louis XVI. But how and when to use this military force was as problematic in Paris in July 1789 as it had been in Grenoble a year before and in countless cities throughout France all through the spring.

At the place Vendôme, matters came to a head. The Prince de Lambesc, commanding a company of the Royal-Allemand stationed in the place Louis XV (shortly to be renamed the place de la Révolution and now the consensually bland space of the place de la Concorde), was ordered to clear the square. Standard procedure was for the cavalry to use the flat of their sabers, but the equally standard consequence was that the horses were surrounded to the point of immobility. Outnumbered, the dragoons retreated to the place Louis XV. From the place Vendôme the crowd ran into the Tuileries gardens. There they collided with troops, and the man who was carrying Curtius's bust of the Duc d'Orléans was dragged behind a horse back to the place Louis XV. As further cavalrymen struggled to get into the gardens, the crowd, shouting '*Au meurtre,*' moved to the balustraded terrace, from where they heaved anything they could down onto the soldiers. Chairs, stones from a construction site, even parts of statues where they could be broken and moved rained down, panicking the horses and wounding the soldiers.

The skirmish went on long enough for word that 'Germans and Swiss are massacring the people' to take wing around the city, and units of the *gardes françaises* arrived on the scene in battle order to confront Lambesc's troopers. It was the first moment that an organized armed force had faced the King's soldiers, determined to counter-attack. More astonishing still, the *gardes* were in sufficient force to push the cavalry troopers out of the Tuileries altogether. From that point, battle was joined for sovereignty over Paris.

For all the weeks of military planning and preparation, first by the Maréchal de Broglie, then by Besenval, it was not much of a battle. It was obvious that the beleaguered company on the place Louis XV needed help, but it was provided by the Swiss Salis-Samade regiment in the most laborious possible manner. As the sun was setting, troops were ferried across the Seine in just two boats, guns mounted in the bows to deter fire from the right bank, where the *gardes françaises* had strengthened their positions. After two hours of this miserable progress, they attempted to re-form in battle order under a night sky of inky darkness. Light came as they were fired on from *gardes françaises* positions on the boulevards. By one o'clock the commander of the Salis-Samade had decided that the position was untenable. When Besenval returned to the scene, he made the even more dramatic decision to evacuate the whole area, retreating westward to the Pont de Sèvres.

The retreat of royal troops from the center of the city delivered it over to haphazard violence. Gunsmiths and armorers were forced to hand over muskets, sabers, pistols and shoulder belts. One master gunsmith later reported to the National Assembly that his shop had been broken into thirty times and had lost 150 swords, 4 gross blades, 58 hunting knives, 10 brace of pistols and 8 muskets.

Armed with this assortment of weapons – as well as kitchen knives, daggers and clubs – crowds at the northern end of the city set about destroying the hated symbol of their confinement: the Farmers'-General wall and its fifty-four *barrières*. The *enceinte* had been Lavoisier's last technical masterpiece, ten feet high, eighteen miles in circumference, punctuated at intervals by Claude Ledoux's extraordinary customs posts. The crowd was not interested in technology or in architecture. The wall meant high prices and brutal police, vexation and starvation. It was breached in several places, then haphazardly torn down, the stones serving as another kind of weapon to be used against troops. Forty of the customs posts were sacked, their doors and furniture burned together with papers and tax records. Among the attackers were fifteen who described themselves (in 1790) as smugglers who, in the euphoria of the moment, as Jacques Godechot has commented, failed to realize they were putting themselves out of business. The crowds were mostly from the northern *faubourgs* and included a number of masons, so that it is a reasonable bet that at least some of those who had helped construct the *enceinte* now joined in pulling it down.

The third target was, of course, bread or, at least, grain and flour. The monastery of Saint-Lazare (the scene of Beaumarchais' humiliation) was not only a prison but a commercial depot. Inevitably it attracted to itself the reputation of being a house full of corpulent monks sitting on immense piles of grain. Crowds, consisting of some of the poorest and hungriest Parisians, put it to the sack and removed any kind of foodstuffs they could find. Large quantities of grain were taken, as were wine, vinegar, oil, twenty-five Gruyère cheeses and, more improbably, a dried ram's head.

During that single night of largely unobstructed riot and demolition, Paris was lost to the monarchy. Only if Besenval was prepared to use his troops the following day to occupy the city and deal brutally with disorder was there any hope of recapture. But the messy, chaotic nocturnal operation had, if anything, unsteadied his grip on command even further. Told by his own officers that their own soldiers, even the Swiss and Germans, could not be counted on, he was unwilling to take the offensive.

On Monday the thirteenth he was faced with a more serious threat than the kind of spontaneous havoc of the day before. At eleven the previous evening there had been a meeting of some of the electors at the Hôtel de Ville. They decided to summon emergency sessions at each of the sixty district headquarters at dawn the following day. The only way this could be announced was by the ringing of the recognized signal for times of peril – the tocsin – and reinforcing the message with cannon shots and the beating of drums. So it was with this thunderous cacophony – the clanging of church bells and the firing of guns – that citizens were summoned to their patriotic duty.

At the Hôtel de Ville the paramount concern was to take control of a situation that threatened to disintegrate into anarchy. The means, as in countless other cities in France, was to form a militia restricted to the electoral elements of the population: those, in other words, with something to lose. Units of eight hundred in each district were to be mobilized, making up in total a citizens' army of forty-eight thousand. Even when allowance had been made for its inevitable inexperience and the need to be guided and trained by the *gardes françaises*, it was an imposing force – substantial enough to perform its twin duties of facing down any further attempt at military repression and containing and, if necessary, punishing unlawful violence. Crucial to the transfer of authority represented in this act was the provision of identifiable insignia. Since uniforms could hardly be provided at short notice, cockades were to be worn on coats and hats. Green was ruled out when it was discovered to be the color not only of hope but the livery of the Comte d'Artois. As an alternative that signified more emphatically the passage of legitimacy, the colors of Paris, red and blue, became the colors of its citizen-soldiers. The official nature of this choice, however, did not preclude more romantic interpretations. In his capacity as poet-Patriot, Desmoulins described the colors of the uniform as red, representing the blood to be shed for freedom, and blue, representing the celestial constitution that would be its eventual blessing. And one of the first to wear the tricolor was Citizen Curtius, who volunteered his services to the militia on the first day of its duty.

Their first munitions did not do much for the dignity of the new militia, though these did provide yet more theatrical color. Ransacking the royal *garde-meuble* near the Tuileries, they extracted antique halberds and pikes, a sword said to have belonged to their folk hero Henri IV and a cannon inlaid with silver that had been presented to Louis XIV by the King of Siam. More serious equipment was harder to lay hands on. Powder had been moved from the Arsenal to the Bastille on Besenval's orders a few days earlier. When the royal *prévôt des marchands*, de Flesselles, was told to hand over weapons from the Hôtel de Ville he could come up with only three muskets. Alternative suggestions proposed by him – the Carthusian monastery by the Luxembourg and the gun factory at Charleville – turned out to be wild-goose chases, so that by the end of the day de Flesselles' own credibility was deeply compromised. He agreed to ask the commandant of the garrison at the Invalides, de Sombreuil, to hand over the thirty thousand muskets at his disposal, but he too procrastinated, replying that he had first to seek permission from Versailles.

Finally, thirty-five casks of powder were produced from a barge at the Port Saint-Nicolas and enough weapons and powder were distributed for patrols that night, the thirteenth. In contrast with the night before, bourgeois sympathizers with the Revolution felt safe enough to go on the streets as they saw the worker-sorties disarmed by the militia. There were even exemplary hangings of looters, and candles and oil lamps once again illuminated houses and streets.

It was early the next morning, with low clouds hanging over Paris, that the battle was won. Dissatisfied with the answer they had received the previous evening, an immense crowd, estimated by some to be eighty thousand strong, converged on the Invalides. Some days before, eighty of their comrades in the Invalides had already jumped the camp and the rest responded with a paralyzing slowdown action to de Sombreuil's order to sabotage the thirty thousand muskets in his barracks. The twenty *invalides* veterans assigned to this job may not have been in their prime but they could probably have done better than unscrewing twenty muskets in six hours had not patriotic enthusiasm caught up with them too. After some fruitless negotiation, weight of numbers forced an entrance and de Sombreuil barely escaped with his life. The garrison helped rather than hindered the invasion and, more seriously, there was no attempt to mobilize the troops nearby on the Champ de Mars. More than thirty thousand muskets were distributed, somewhat at random, as well as cannon (which had also been inadequately spiked).

It was not quite a conclusive victory. For despite the evidence of defection among some troops and the inertia of their commanders, there were still rumors that, before long, regiments would be on the march and cannon would sound from Montmartre. What use were muskets and cannon without powder? By now it was widely known where the powder was to be had that would make the citizens' army invincible in Paris: from the Bastille. It only remained to go and get it.

Buried Alive? Myths and Realities in the Bastille

The Bastille had an address. It was identified as No. 232, rue Saint-Antoine, as if it were some overgrown lodging house, full of *chambres garnies* and guests of different quality occupying rooms that varied according to their means and station. Its exterior court (except during the July rising) was open to the public, who could come and chat to the gatekeeper (who sat in the little lodge), lounge around the shops that crowded at its entrance or inspect the progress of the governor's vegetable garden.

But it was also a fortress. Eight round towers, each with walls five feet thick, rose above the Arsenal and the *faubourg*. Paintings that celebrated the fall and demolition of the Bastille invariably made it look taller than it really was. The highest of the irregularly built towers was no more than seventy-three feet, but Hubert Robert, a specialist in the grandeur of ruins, gave it Babylonian eminence. In his painting, those walls became monstrous clifflike ramparts that could have been conquered only by the superhuman courage and will of the People.

Like so many others of its initial enthusiasts, Hubert Robert would himself end up a prisoner of the Revolution. But in 1789 he was already a devotee of

Romantic aesthetics: the swooping emotions of the Sublime and the Terrible outlined in Edmund Burke's first great publication. His great visual mentor was Giambattista Piranesi, whom he followed in offering views of the masonry of antiquity fallen into picturesque decay. Perhaps, then, he also shared Piranesi's nightmare, the *carceri d'invenzione:* prisons of the mind in which the mechanical genius of the modern age was applied to the science of confinement and pain. Certainly the elevation of the Bastille in his painting, with tiny figures scampering jubilantly over its battlements, suggests an immense Gothic castle of darkness and secrecy, a place into which men would disappear without warning and never again see the light of day until their bones were disinterred by revolutionary excavators.

That was the legend of the Bastille. Its reality was far more prosaic. Constructed at the end of the fourteenth century as a defense against the English, it had been converted into a state prison by Charles VI. It was Cardinal Richelieu, though, who gave it its sinister reputation as a place into which prisoners of state were spirited away. Throughout the reign of the Bourbons, most, though not all, of its prisoners were detained by *lettres de cachet* at the express warrant of the King and without any kind of judicial process. From the beginning, many of them were high-born: conspirators against the crown and its Ministers; others were religious prisoners, Protestants and, in the early eighteenth century, Catholic 'convulsionaries' accused of fomenting heresy. There were two other important categories of detainees. The first were writers whose works were declared seditious and a danger either to public decency or order or both; the second were delinquents, usually young, whose families had petitioned the King for their incarceration.

Conditions varied widely. The infamous subterranean *cachots*, slimy with damp and overrun with vermin, were no longer in use by the reign of Louis XVI, but the *calottes* immediately below the roof were almost as bad, since they took in snow and rain in the winter and almost asphyxiated prisoners with heat in the summer. For the majority of prisoners, however, conditions were by no means as bad as in other prisons, in particular the horrors that prevailed at Bicêtre. (For that matter, compared with what twentieth-century tyrannies have provided, the Bastille was paradise.) Sums were allotted to the governor for the subsistence of different ranks: fifteen livres a day for *conseillers* of the Parlement, nine for *bourgeois* and three for commoners. Paradoxically, 'men of letters,' who created the myth of a fortress of atrocities, were allotted the highest sum of nineteen livres a day. Even granting that the governor and his *service* undoubtedly made a profit on these allowances, they were considerably above the level at which most of the population of France attempted to subsist.

Most prisoners were held in octagonal rooms, about sixteen feet in diameter, in middle levels of the five- to seven-storied towers. Under Louis XVI they each had a bed with green serge curtains, one or two tables and several chairs. All had a stove or chimney, and in many rooms prisoners were able to ascend to a triple-barred window by a three-stepped staircase against the wall.

Many were permitted to bring in their own possessions and to keep dogs or cats to deal with the vermin. The Marquis de Sade, who was held there until the week before the Bastille fell, took full advantage of these privileges. He brought in (among other things) a desk, wardrobe, *nécessaire* for his dressing needs; a full complement of shirts, silk breeches, *frac* coats in camel-brown, dressing gowns, several pairs of boots and shoes; his favorite firedogs and tongs; four family portraits, tapestries to hang on the white plaster walls; velvet cushions and pillows, mattresses to make the bed more comfortable; a selection of hats; three fragrances – rose water, orange water and eau-de-cologne – with which to anoint himself and plenty of candles and oil night lamps. These were necessary since on admission in 1784 he also brought in a library of 133 volumes, including Hume's histories, the complete works of Fénelon, novels by Fielding and Smollett, the *Iliad*, the plays of Marmontel, travel literature about and by Cook and Bougainville in the South Seas as well as an *Histoire des Filles Célèbres* and the *Danger d'Aimer Etranger*.

If there ever was a justification for the Bastille, it was the Marquis de Sade. But if the crimes which put him there were unusually disgusting (by the standards of any century), his living conditions were not. He received visits from his long-suffering wife almost weekly and when his eyes deteriorated from both reading and writing, oculists came to see him on a regular basis. Like others in the 'Liberty' tower, he could walk in the walled garden courtyard and on the towers. Only when he abused that right by shouting cheerful or indignant obscenities to passersby (which he did with increasing frequency in 1789) was it curtailed.

Food – that crucial event in the lives of prisoners – also varied according to social condition. The commoners detained in connection with the 'flour war' riots of 1775 were probably fed gruels and soups, sometimes lined with a string of bacon or lardy ham. But even they had a decent provision of bread, wine and cheese. It was not necessary to be a noble, though, to enjoy a much better cuisine. The writer Marmontel drooled when he recalled 'an excellent soup, a succulent side of beef, a thigh of boiled chicken oozing with grease [an eighteenth-century compliment]; a little dish of fried, marinaded artichokes or of spinach; really fine Cressane pears; fresh grapes, a bottle of old Burgundy and the best Moka coffee.'

No one wanted to be in the Bastille. But once there, life for the more privileged could be made bearable. Alcohol and tobacco were allowed, and under Louis XVI card games were introduced for anyone sharing a cell as well as a billiard table for the Breton gentry who requested one. Some of the literary inmates even thought a spell in the Bastille established their credentials as a true foe of despotism. The Abbé Morellet, for example, wrote, 'I saw literary glory illuminate the walls of my prison. Once persecuted I would be better known . . . and those six months of the Bastille would be an excellent recommendation and infallibly make my fortune.'

Morellet's admission suggests that as the reality of the Bastille became more of an anachronism, its demonology became more and more important in defining opposition to state power. If the monarchy was to be depicted (not completely without justice) as arbitrary, obsessed with secrecy and vested with capricious powers over the life and death of its citizens, the Bastille was the perfect symbol of those vices. If it had not existed, it is safe to say, it would have had to be invented.

And in some senses it *was* reinvented by a succession of writings of prisoners who had indeed suffered within its walls but whose account of the institution transcended anything they could have experienced. So vivid and haunting were their accounts that they succeeded in creating a stark opposition around which critics of the regime could rally. The Manichean opposition between incarceration and liberty; secrecy and candor; torture and humanity; depersonalization and individuality; open-air and shut-in obscurity were all basic elements of the Romantic language in which the anti-Bastille literature expressed itself. The critique was so powerful that when the fortress was taken, the anti-climactic reality of liberating a mere seven prisoners (including two lunatics, four forgers and an aristocratic delinquent who had been committed with de Sade) was not allowed to intrude on mythic expectations. Revolutionary propaganda remade the Bastille's history, in text, image and object, to conform more fully to the inspirational myth.

The 1780s were the great age of prison literature. Hardly a year went by without another contribution to the genre, usually bearing the title *The Bastille Revealed* (La Bastille Dévoilée) or some variation. It used the standard Gothic devices of provoking shudders of disgust and fear together with pulse-accelerating moments of hope. In particular, as Monique Cottret has pointed out, it drew on the fashionable terror of being buried alive. This was such a preoccupation in the late eighteenth century (and not only in France) that it was possible to join societies that would guarantee to send a member to one's burial to listen for signs and sounds of vitality and to insure against one of these living entombments.

In what was by far the greatest and deservedly the most popular of all the anti-Bastille books, Linguet's *Memoirs of the Bastille*, the prison was depicted as just such a living tomb. In some of its most powerful passages Linguet represented captivity as a death, all the worse for the officially extinguished person being fully conscious of his own obliteration.

Linguet's memoir burned with the heat of personal betrayal. He had, he said, been lured back to France in 1780 from England, where he had been publishing his *Annales Politiques*, on the express understanding that he would, in effect, be immune from prosecution. Almost as soon as he returned, he was whisked off to the Bastille because of his attack on the Maréchal Duras. His account of the physical conditions he endured is far more harrowing than anything experienced by Morellet, Marmontel or de Sade and is not altogether borne out by the Bastille archives. But there is no reason to assume he lied when he wrote of 'two mattresses eaten by worms; a cane chair of which the seat had but a few strings holding it together, a folding table . . . two china pots, one to drink from, and two paving stones to hold a fire.' (Some time later the warders brought him some fire irons and tongs – though not, he complained, brass dogs.) His worst moments came when the eggs of mites and moths hatched out and all his bed and personal linen was transformed into 'clouds of butterflies.'

However squalid these conditions, it was the mental rather than the physical ordeal of imprisonment that caused Linguet the most suffering and which he communicates with astonishing originality in his little book. The memoir is, in fact, the first account of prison psychology in Western culture and for the modern reader has a kind of prophetic power that still makes it disturbing reading. Michel Foucault was quite wrong in assuming that the categorization of prisoners was one of the techniques which was most repressive. For Linguet objected most strenuously to exactly the lack of such a categorization. 'The Bastille, like death itself,' he lamented, 'equalizes all whom it engulfs: the sacrilegious who have meditated on the ruin of their *patrie* as well as the courageous man who is guilty only of having defended his rights with excessive ardor' (that is, himself). Worst of all was having to share the same space with those confined for moral abominations.

Everything about the regime of the prison, even when it seemed, superficially, to take the edge off brutality, appeared part of a sinister design to strip the prisoner of his identity: the 'I' which for Romantics was synonymous with life itself. On admission, for example, potentially dangerous objects – a category which included both scissors and money – were confiscated and inventoried, to be returned on release, exactly like modern procedure. The reasons for these confiscations were read out to the prisoner, a business which Linguet found deliberately humiliating: the systematic reduction of a rational adult to the dependency of a child. He found that condition reinforced by all manner of petty tyrannies, such as being obliged to have an escort while being exercised in the little high-walled yard.

Even worse was the inability to communicate, particularly galling for a writer and terrible in captivity of indeterminate length. Seized without warning – and usually at night – from the living world, the victim of this state abduction was then deprived of all means of communicating his existence to friends or family beyond the walls. For most prisoners this was not in fact a problem, but for some time Linguet was deprived of writing materials and it was this helplessness that most oppressed him. The massive thickness of the walls, which made it impossible to speak to, or hear, other prisoners or indeed even summon a doctor in case of sudden sickness, only added to the sense of live burial. The walls of the Bastille then became the frontier between being and nonexistence. When the prison barber was brought to him, Linguet made the grim quip that became famous: '*Hé*, Monsieur, you wield a razor? Why don't you raze the Bastille?'

The Man Who Loved Rats

If Linguet was the writer who enabled the thousands who read his book to feel, vicariously, the shutting out of light, another, quite different but equally popular book gave its readers the elation of escape. In this sense, the 'Chevalier' Latude's autobiography was the perfect complement to Linguet's memoir.

'Latude' was in reality a soldier named Danry who found himself without means or prospects in Paris after the end of the War of Austrian Succession. Like countless petty adventurers, he attempted to use the machinery of court favoritism to advance himself but he did so with an unconventionally risky stratagem. In 1750 he wrote a personal letter to Mme de Pompadour – the object of countless personal plots – alerting her to a letter bomb that would shortly be sent her way. Danry/Latude could be confident of this because he himself was the author of just such a letter. The half-baked plan was very quickly unraveled, and instead of receiving a pension in gratitude for saving the life of the King's mistress, Latude found himself in the Bastille. Transferred after a few months to Vincennes, he made the first of what was to be a series of escapes.

Latude's account of his first moments of freedom, running through fields and vineyards, making for the highway, hiding away in a *chambre garnie* in Paris, has exhilarating credibility. But even more astonishing was his decision to extricate himself from the fear of discovery by writing again to Mme de Pompadour, explaining his folly and throwing himself on her mercy. Since he had become acquainted with no less an eminence than Dr. Quesnay, he entrusted him with this apologetic memorandum.

This was a serious mistake. Latude had been so naively confident of clemency that he had even indicated his address on the letter. Within a day or so he was back in the Bastille: a setback but not a defeat. The innocent was rapidly becoming accustomed to the cunning of the world. Within a few months he had devised a secret mailbox by working loose a brick in the prison chapel, and he with a cellmate, d'Alègre, spent six months constructing the rope ladder that would take him to freedom again. This extraordinary piece of work required considerable sacrifice since the rungs had to be made from the firewood given to the prisoners during the winter. Shirts and bed linen, torn apart, knotted and restitched with painstaking care, made up the length. A crude knife was fashioned from the iron crossbar of their trestle table. With his passion for giving sacred names to the instruments of freedom (also a precaution against discovery) Latude called the runged ladder 'Jacob,' the white rope his 'dove.' In his memoir he represents himself as the perfect artisan: frugal, industrious, ingenious and pure of heart – Jean-Jacques as convict.

On the night of the twenty-fifth of February the two prisoners climbed up the chimney of their cell, 'almost suffocating from soot and nearly burned alive,' then worked the iron grate apart to allow them onto the roof of one of the towers. From there they used the three-hundred-foot ladder to descend into one of the moats. It was here, said Latude, that he felt a pang of regret at having to abandon his tools and the ladder that had served him so well: 'rare and precious monuments of human industry and the virtues that were the outcome of the love of liberty.' The two men were still not free. The rain on which they had counted to remove the sentries had stopped and they were making their rounds as usual, armed with broad lanterns. The only way out was to work from below, removing the bricks of a wall, one by one, with a minimum of noise, to allow for an eventual exit. And when they finally had made a hole large enough to squeeze through, the two men, in the dark, fell headlong into an aqueduct and were nearly drowned.

After this ordeal they were hidden for a time in the Abbaye Saint-Germain by a tailor before going their separate ways through the Low Countries. In Antwerp, Latude encountered a Savoyard who, without blinking, recited to him the story of two men who had escaped from the Bastille. One of them, he said, had already been recaptured and the 'exempts' – police who moved freely across borders – were out looking for the other. In Amsterdam they caught up with Latude and, tied into a dreadful leather harness 'more humiliating than any slave's,' he was taken back to the Bastille. His liberty had lasted just three months.

This time the jailbird's wings were clipped. Latude was placed in one of the appalling underground *cachots* to make escape quite impossible. And it was in this genuinely nightmarish confinement that he discovered new companions: the rats. Compared with the inhumanity Latude had endured, the rats seemed endearing. Using pieces of bread he trained them to eat off his plate and to allow him to scratch them around the neck and chin. They too were given names, and some, like the female 'Rapino-hirondelle,' would even beg like a dog or do jumping tricks for her pieces of bread. The scene of an idyll in hell was completed when Latude managed to make a primitive flute out of bits of his iron grille so that, from time to time, he could serenade his rodent friends with an air or a gavotte as they gnawed contentedly on his leavings. They were, as he wrote, his 'little family,' all twenty-six of them, and Latude studiously observed their life cycle – their matings and breedings, battles and games – with all the tender concern of Rousseau's guardian-tutor.

Years passed. Latude busied himself by preparing a project reforming the halberdiers and pikemen in the French army, which he was sure the Minister of War would want to see. Deprived of paper he used tablets of bread, moistened and flattened with his saliva and then dried, and for ink his own blood diluted with water. When he was hauled out of the *cachot*, he grieved to lose his rats but made a new family out of the pigeons, until in a vindictive fit they were killed on orders from the governor. Another escape was made in 1765, aborted again through Latude's incurable innocence when he presented himself at the Versailles office of a government minister whose reputation for benevolence he trusted. He was moved back to the Château de Vincennes, and it was only in the new reign that Malesherbes became acquainted with his plight and had him moved to Charenton, the asylum for the mentally disturbed. There he met up again with d'Alègre, his old companion in flight, whose years of incarceration had completely destroyed his sanity. Seeing Latude, d'Alègre thought he was God and covered him with tears and benedictions.

In 1777 Latude was finally released but immediately published his *Memoirs of Vengeance*, which guaranteed his rearrest, first in the Petit Châtelet and then in Bicêtre. From there he continued to write accounts of his many ordeals, one of which found its way to a poor vendor of pamphlets and magazines, Mme Legros. Campaigning for Latude at the doors of *les Grands* she finally found a willing audience in Mme Necker and even the Queen. In March 1784 Latude was finally released, and though he was formally 'exiled' from Paris he was not only permitted to live there but was given a royal pension of four hundred livres a year. Unlike d'Alègre Latude had somehow come through twenty-eight years of prison with his wits very much intact, and he became an immediate celebrity. Lionized by the Académie Française, greeted by Jefferson, he became the beneficiary of a public fund.

Latude's story, published in many forms and editions before the Revolution, looked like the triumph of the *honnête homme* over the worst miseries that despotism could inflict. Together with Linguet's memoir and other writings like *The Bastille Revealed*, it contributed to a growing campaign, first to restrict *lettres de cachet* and

summary imprisonment to those who genuinely threatened the public peace, and then to demolish the Bastille
altogether. Such plans were in keeping with plans of
urban embellishment that removed medieval walls and
citadels to make room for public gardens, squares and
promenades. In 1784, as an accompaniment to Breteuil's
memorandum limiting the use of *lettres de cachet*, the
architect Brogniard proposed an open, circular, colonnaded space and in June 1789 the project was revived by
the Royal Academy of Architecture.

Just a few weeks before it fell to the citizens' army,
then, the Bastille had already been demolished in official
memoranda. In the broad open space to be created by
its removal would be a column, perhaps in bronze,
higher than the old prison. Its base was to be sheathed
in rocks from which fountains would play, in keeping
with the new Romantic aesthetic. A simple inscription
would suffice to indicate to posterity the victory of benevolence over tyranny: 'Louis XVI, Restorer of Public
Freedom.'

This peaceful victory was not to be. The attempt of
the monarchy to impose its will by military force had
ended any possibility of recasting its legitimacy as the
benefactor of freedom. Instead, the towers of the
Bastille, its cannon pointing from the embrasures, stood
as the symbol of intransigence. So, although, as histor-
ians never tire of pointing out, the crowd of a thousand
that gathered before its front court was after gunpowder rather than demolition, it was, without any ques-
tion, also mobilized by the immense force of the
Bastille's evil mystique.

The Marquis de Sade, for one, knew exactly how to exploit this. Briefed by his wife during her weekly visits on all the news from Versailles, he decided to join the roll of honorable martyrs of the Bastille. His periodically shouted addresses from the tower walks to passersby suddenly became political at the beginning of July. Deprived of those walks, he followed the tradition of artisanal ingenuity in the Bastille by adapting into an improvised megaphone the metal funnel used to deposit his urine and slops into the moat. From de Sade's window, at regular intervals, like news bulletins on the hour, came broadcast announcements to the effect that Governor de Launay planned a massacre of all the prisoners; that they were at this minute being massacred and that the People should deliver them before it was too late. Already in a state of jitters, de Launay had the troublemaker removed on about the fifth of July to Charenton, where he raged at the indignity of being shut up with so many epileptics and lunatics.

De Sade had become a revolutionary.

The Fourteenth of July 1789

Bernard-René de Launay had been born in the Bastille, where his father had been governor, and he would die on the evening of the fourteenth of July in the shadow of its towers. The aristocratic revolutionary de Sade sneered at the '*soi-disant* marquis whose grandfather was a *valet-de-chambre*.' The truth was that the governor was a typical minor functionary of the old regime, reasonably conscientious if somewhat dour; certainly an improvement on martinets like Governor de Berryer, who had made Latude's life so wretched.

On the fourteenth of July he was, with good reason, apprehensive. By default the entire integrity of royal authority in Paris seemed to have devolved on him. The Baron de Besenval had virtually evacuated the center of the city. The commandant of the Invalides had sent him the huge consignment of 250 barrels of powder (about thirty thousand pounds), yet he had only a modest force with which to defend it. In response to an urgent request for reinforcements, he had been given, on July 7, a further thirty-two men from the Swiss Salis-Samade regiment to add to the eighty-two *invalides* pensioners stationed there. Well known in the *faubourg* as amiable layabouts, the *invalides* were unlikely to defend the fortress to the last man. Worst of all, in the event of siege, the Bastille had only a two-day supply of food and no internal supply of water at all. In the end, that was what probably decided its capitulation.

In front of the outer courtyard were gathered about nine hundred Parisians. They included a few men of standing and property like Santerre, a friend of Réveillon's who owned the famous Hortensia Brewery, which specialized in the English-style ales and stouts that were in great demand in the capital. There were also a sizable number of defecting soldiers and *gardes françaises*. But making up by far the largest number were local artisans living in the faubourg Saint-Antoine – joiners, cabinetmakers, hatters, locksmiths, cobblers, tailors and the like. There were also a good number – twenty-one according to the official list of the *vainqueurs de la Bastille* – of wine merchants, which is to say owners of the *cabarets* that served as well as sold wine and which were the headquarters of neighborhood gossip and politics. One of them, Claude Cholat, whose wine shop was in the rue Noyer, produced a justly famous 'primitive' graphic rendering of the day's events. Of the six hundred of whom we have information, as many as four hundred in the crowd had immigrated to Paris from the provinces, and since July 14 saw the price of the four-pound loaf reach a record high, most of their families were undoubtedly hungry.

They were also prey to considerable fear. During the night rumors had circulated that troops were about to march or were already on their way from Sèvres and Saint-Denis to crush the Paris rising. And the Bastille seemed to be heavily munitioned, with fifteen eight-pounder cannon on the towers and a further three in the inner courtyard pointing at the gates. Twelve more guns on the ramparts could fire pound-and-a-half balls, and in his nervousness de Launay had even assembled a bizarre collection of siege missiles like paving stones and rusty ironmongery to drop on the assailants, should that be necessary.

The initial aim of the crowd was simply to neutralize the guns and to take possession of the powder. To this end, two delegates from the Hôtel de Ville asked to see the governor, and since it was around ten in the morning they were invited in for *déjeuner*. Even by the standards of the last day of the *ancien régime*, this seemed a lengthy entertainment. The crowd, from the beginning, had been suspicious when de Launay had refused entry to any but the two delegates and had demanded three 'hostage' soldiers in exchange. The prolonged lunch combined with some indeterminate business around the rampart guns (in fact their withdrawal from the embrasures) deepened those suspicions. A second deputy, Thuriot de La Rozière, was sent for from the district headquarters of Saint-Louis-la-Culture, and he too was admitted to see de Launay, this time armed with specific instructions. The guns, along with their powder, should be removed and delivered to the militia representing the city of Paris, and a unit of the militia should be admitted to the Bastille. This, de Launay replied, was impossible until he had received instructions from Versailles, but he took Thuriot up to the ramparts to inspect the withdrawal of the guns.

It was about half past twelve. Not much had been achieved on either side. None of the essential demands

made by Thuriot had been granted, and although he
had made efforts to persuade the *invalides* to come to
some agreement with the people, de Launay's officers
had insisted that it would be dishonorable to hand over
the fortress without express orders from their seniors.
Thuriot decided to report back to the electors at the
Hôtel de Ville for further negotiating instructions. They
were themselves reluctant to inflame the situation, and
at half past one Thuriot was about to return to the
Bastille with another elector, Ethis de Corny, equipped
with bugle and loud-hailer by which the removal of the
guns would be announced to the people, when the Hôtel
de Ville shook to the sound of an explosion followed
by the crackle of musket fire coming from the fort.

While he had been gone, the impatience of the crowd
had finally burst its bounds. Shouts of 'Give us the
Bastille' were heard, and the nine hundred had pressed
into the undefended outer courtyard, becoming angrier
by the minute. A group, including an ex-soldier now
carriage maker, had climbed onto the roof of a perfume
shop abutting the gate to the inner courtyard and, fail-
ing to find the keys to the courtyard, had cut the drawbridge chains. They had crashed down without warning,
killing one of the crowd who stood beneath, and over
the bridge and his body poured hundreds of the
besiegers. At this point the defending soldiers shouted
to the people to withdraw or else they would fire, and
this too was misinterpreted as encouragement to come
further. The first shots were fired. Subsequently each
side would claim the other fired first, but since no one
among the melee knew that their own people had cut

the drawbridge, it was assumed that they had been let into the inner courtyard in order to be mowed down in the confined space by the cannon.

It was of a piece with all the other assumptions of treachery and conspiracy – of the cordial greeting behind which was the plan of death and destruction. Artois and those responsible for Necker's removal; de Flesselles, who had sent the arms searchers on wild-goose chases; the Queen, who appeared tender-hearted yet plotted revenge were all among this cast of villains as far as the people were concerned. And now de Launay, the governor who let down the drawbridge to take better aim, joined their number. It was the fury unleashed by this 'deceit' that made it impossible for subsequent delegations from the electors (of which there were many) to get past the fighting and organize some kind of cease-fire.

The battle became serious. At about half past three in the afternoon the crowd was reinforced by companies of *gardes françaises* and by defecting soldiers, including a number who were veterans of the American campaign. Two in particular, Second-Lieutenant Jacob Elie, the standard-bearer of the Infantry of the Queen, and Pierre-Augustin Hulin, the director of the Queen's laundry, were crucial in turning the incoherent assault into an organized siege. Like a number of key participants in the events of 1789, Hulin had been a Genevan revolutionary in 1782, and on encountering Mme de Staël the previous day had sworn to 'avenge your father on those bastards who are trying to kill us,' a promise she may or may not have found gratifying.

Hulin and Elie also brought an ample supply of arms taken from the Invalides that morning. With them were two cannon, one bronze and the other the Siamese gun inlaid with silver that had been seized from the royal storehouse the day before. It was Louis XIV's toy, then, that would end the old regime in Paris.

It was decided to aim the guns directly at the gate (since balls seemed to bounce harmlessly off the eight-foot-thick walls). Before that could be done, carts filled with burning dung and straw, which had been lit by Santerre to provide smoke cover for the movements of the besiegers, had to be removed from the approach to the gate. At some risk to himself Elie did this in company with a haberdasher familiarly known as 'Vive l'Amour.' The heavy guns were drawn back on gun carriages, charged and aimed.

A wooden gate now divided the cannon of the besiegers from those of the defenders – perhaps a hundred feet apart. Had they opened up at each other, dreadful carnage would have been guaranteed. But if the attackers could not see the defending guns, the defending troops were well aware of the peril they stood in. Faced with the increasing reluctance of the *invalides* to prolong the fighting, de Launay was himself demoralized. In any case, there was no food with which to withstand a prolonged siege, so that his main concern now was for a surrender that would preserve the honor and the lives of the garrison. He had one card – the powder. In his darkest moments he simply thought of exploding the entire store – and destroying a large part of the faubourg Saint-Antoine – rather

than capitulating. Dissuaded from this act of desperation, he resolved to use the threat at least to secure an
honorable evacuation.

With no white flag available, a handkerchief was
flown from one of the towers and the Bastille's guns
stopped firing. At around five, a note asking for such a
capitulation, written by the governor – and threatening
the explosion unless it was given – was stuck through
a chink in the drawbridge wall of the inner courtyard.
A plank was laid down over the moat with men standing on one end to steady it. The first person on the
plank fell into the moat but the second – whose identity thereafter was hotly disputed retrieved it. The
demand, however, was refused, and in response to the
continued anger of the crowd Hulin was apparently
preparing to fire the Siamese cannon when the drawbridge suddenly came down.

The *vainqueurs* rushed into the prison, liberated all
seven of the prisoners, took possession of the gunpowder
and disarmed the defending troops. The Swiss guards,
who had prudently taken off their uniform coats, were
initially mistaken for prisoners and unharmed. But some
of the *invalides* were brutally dealt with. A soldier named
Béquard, who had been one of those responsible for
dissuading de Launay from detonating the gunpowder,
had his hand severed almost as soon as he opened one
of the gates of the fort. Under the impression that he
was one of the prison warders, the crowd paraded the
hand about the streets still gripping a key. Later that
evening he was misidentified again, this time as one of
the cannoneers who had first fired on the people, and

was hanged in the place de Grève, along with one of his comrades, before the thirty Swiss guards lined up as an obligatory audience.

The battle itself had taken the lives of eighty-three of the citizens' army. Another fifteen were to die from wounds. Only one of the *invalides* had died in the fighting and three had been wounded. The imbalance was enough for the crowd to demand some sort of punitive sacrifice, and de Launay duly provided it. All of the hatred which to a large degree had been spared the garrison was concentrated on him. His attributes of command – a sword and baton – were wrenched away from him and he was marched towards the Hôtel de Ville through enormous crowds, all of whom were convinced he had been foiled in a diabolical plot to massacre the people. Hulin and Elie managed to prevent the crowd from killing him on the street, though more than once he was knocked down and badly beaten. Throughout the walk he was covered in abuse and spittle. Outside the Hôtel de Ville competing suggestions were offered as to how he should meet his end, including a proposal to tie him to a horse's tail and drag him over the cobbles. A pastry cook named Desnot said it would be better to take him into the Hôtel de Ville – but at that point de Launay, who had had enough of the ordeal, shouted 'Let me die' and lashed out with his boots, landing a direct hit in Desnot's groin. He was instantaneously covered with darting knives, swords and bayonets, rolled to the gutter and finished off with a barrage of pistol shots.

The Revolution in Paris had begun with heads hoisted

aloft over the crowd. They had been the heads of heroes, made in wax, carried as proxy commanders. It needed a symmetrical ending: more heads, this time serving as trophies of battle. A sword was handed to Desnot, but he cast it aside and used a pocketknife to saw through de Launay's neck. A little later, de Flesselles, the *prévôt des marchands* who had also been accused of deliberately misleading the people about stores of arms, was shot as he emerged from the Hôtel de Ville. The heads were stuck on pikes that bobbed and dipped above cheering, laughing and singing crowds that filled the streets.

Nine days later there were two more heads to display: those of Bertier de Sauvigny, the *intendant* of Paris, and Foulon, one of the ministers in the government that was to have replaced Necker's. The latter was accused of the famine plot, so the mouth of his severed head was crammed with grass, straw and ordure to signify his particular crime. The young painter Girodet thought this popular symbolism so picturesque that he made a careful sketch as the heads passed before him.

More than the actual casualties of fighting (which, as we have seen, were very limited), it was this display of punitive sacrifice that constituted a kind of revolutionary sacrament. Some, who had celebrated the Revolution so long as it was expressed in abstractions like *Liberté*, gagged at the sight of blood thrust in their faces. Others whose nerves were tougher and stomachs less easily turned made the modern compact by which power could be secured through violence. The beneficiaries of this bargain deluded themselves into believing that they could turn it on and off like a faucet and direct its force with exacting selectivity. Barnave, the Grenoble politician who in 1789 was among the unreserved zealots of the National Assembly, was asked whether the deaths of Foulon and Bertier were really necessary to secure freedom. He gave the reply which, converted into an instrument of the revolutionary state, would be the entitlement to kill him on the guillotine:

'What, then, is their blood so pure?'

POCKET PENGUINS

1. Lady Chatterley's Trial
2. **Eric Schlosser** Cogs in the Great Machine
3. **Nick Hornby** Otherwise Pandemonium
4. **Albert Camus** Summer in Algiers
5. **P. D. James** Innocent House
6. **Richard Dawkins** The View from Mount Improbable
7. **India Knight** On Shopping
8. **Marian Keyes** Nothing Bad Ever Happens in Tiffany's
9. **Jorge Luis Borges** The Mirror of Ink
10. **Roald Dahl** A Taste of the Unexpected
11. **Jonathan Safran Foer** The Unabridged Pocketbook of Lightning
12. **Homer** The Cave of the Cyclops
13. **Paul Theroux** Two Stars
14. **Elizabeth David** Of Pageants and Picnics
15. **Anaïs Nin** Artists and Models
16. **Antony Beevor** Christmas at Stalingrad
17. **Gustave Flaubert** The Desert and the Dancing Girls
18. **Anne Frank** The Secret Annexe
19. **James Kelman** Where I Was
20. **Hari Kunzru** Noise
21. **Simon Schama** The Bastille Falls
22. **William Trevor** The Dressmaker's Child
23. **George Orwell** In Defence of English Cooking
24. **Michael Moore** Idiot Nation
25. **Helen Dunmore** Rose, 1944
26. **J. K. Galbraith** The Economics of Innocent Fraud
27. **Gervase Phinn** The School Inspector Calls
28. **W. G. Sebald** Young Austerlitz
29. **Redmond O'Hanlon** Borneo and the Poet
30. **Ali Smith** Ali Smith's Supersonic 70s
31. **Sigmund Freud** Forgetting Things
32. **Simon Armitage** King Arthur in the East Riding
33. **Hunter S. Thompson** Happy Birthday, Jack Nicholson
34. **Vladimir Nabokov** Cloud, Castle, Lake
35. **Niall Ferguson** 1914: Why the World Went to War

POCKET PENGUINS